Laboratories of the Spirit

Laboratories of the Spirit

R. Ronald S. THOMAS

David R. Godine
Boston

First published in 1976 by
David R. Godine, Publisher
306 Dartmouth Street
Boston, Massachusetts

ISBN 0–87923–172–6
LCC 75–18810

Printed in Great Britain

CONTENTS

EMERGING

Not as in the old days I pray,
God. My life is not what it was.
Yours, too, accepts the presence of
the machine? Once I would have asked
healing. I go now to be doctored,
to drink sinlessly of the blood
of my brother, to lend my flesh
as manuscript of the great poem
of the scalpel. I would have knelt
long, wrestling with you, wearing
you down. Hear my prayer, Lord, hear
my prayer. As though you were deaf, myriads
of mortals have kept up their shrill
cry, explaining your silence by
their unfitness.
                  It begins to appear
this is not what prayer is about.
It is the annihilation of difference,
the consciousness of myself in you,
of you in me; the emerging
from the adolescence of nature
into the adult geometry
of the mind. I begin to recognize
you anew, God of form and number.
There are questions we are the solution
to, others whose echoes we must expand
to contain. Circular as our way
is, it leads not back to that snake-haunted
garden, but onward to the tall city
of glass that is the laboratory of the spirit.

THE HAND

It was a hand. God looked at it
and looked away. There was a coldness
about his heart, as though the hand
clasped it. As at the end
of a dark tunnel, he saw cities
the hand would build, engines
that it would raze them with. His sight
dimmed. Tempted to undo the joints
of the fingers, he picked it up.
But the hand wrestled with him. 'Tell
me your name,' it cried, 'and I will write it
in bright gold. Are there not deeds
to be done, children to make, poems
to be written? The world
is without meaning, awaiting
my coming.' But God, feeling the nails
in his side, the unnerving warmth
of the contact, fought on in
silence. This was the long war with himself
always foreseen, the question not
to be answered. What is the hand
for? The immaculate conception
preceding the delivery
of the first tool? 'I let you go,'
he said, 'but without blessing.
Messenger to the mixed things
of your making, tell them I am.'

THE WORD

A pen appeared, and the god said:
'Write what it is to be
man.' And my hand hovered
long over the bare page,

until there, like footprints
of the lost traveller, letters
took shape on the page's
blankness, and I spelled out

the word 'lonely'. And my hand moved
to erase it; but the voices
of all those waiting at life's
window cried out loud: 'It is true.'

OUT THERE

It is another country.
There is no speech there such
as we know; even the colours

                        are different.
When the residents use their eyes,
it is not shapes they see but the distance
between them. If they go,
it is not in a traveller's
usual direction, but sideways and
out through the mirror of a refracted
timescale. If you met them early,
you would recognize them by an absence
of shadow. Your problems

                        are in their past;
those they are about to solve
are what you are incapable
of conceiving. In experiments
in outbreeding, under the growing microscope
of the mind, they are isolating
the human virus and burning it
up in the fierceness of their detachment.

AMEN

It was all arranged:
the virgin with child, the birth
in Bethlehem, the arid journey uphill
to Jerusalem. The prophets foretold
it, the scriptures conditioned him
to accept it. Judas went to his work
with his sour kiss; what else
could he do?
                    A wise old age,
the honours awarded for lasting,
are not for a saviour. He had
to be killed; salvation acquired
by an increased guilt. The tree,
with its roots in the mind's dark,
was divinely planted, the original fork
in existence. There is no meaning in life,
unless men can be found to reject
love. God needs his martyrdom.
The mild eyes stare from the Cross
in perverse triumph. What does he care
that the people's offerings are so small?

WELSH SUMMER

They blow on their horns;
the valleys are full of echoes;
voices from vanished kingdoms
answer them from their recesses
in time. Here there is no sleep
for the dead; they are resurrected
to mourn. Everywhere is the sad
chorus of an old people, waking to weep.

It is the machine wins;
the land suffers the formication
of its presence. Places that
would have preferred peace
have had their bowels opened; our
children paddle thoughtlessly there in the mess.

GOD'S STORY

A thousand years went by.
The Buddha sat under the Bo tree
rhyming. God burned in the sky

as of old. The family waited
for him who would not come back
any more. Who is my father

and mother? God fingered the hole
in his side, where the green tree
came from. The desert gave up

its saints. The Pope's ring was deadly
as a snake's kiss. Art and poetry
drank of that slow poison. God,

looking into a dry chalice,
felt the cold touch of the machine
on his hand, leading him

to a steel altar. 'Where are you?'
he called, seeking himself among
the dumb cogs and tireless camshafts.

THAT PLACE

I served on a dozen committees;
talked hard, said little, shared the applause
at the end. Picking over
the remains later, we agreed power
was not ours, launched our invective
at others, the anonymous wielders
of such. Life became small, grey,
the smell of interiors. Occasions
on which a clean air entered our nostrils
off swept seas were instances
we sought to recapture. One particular
time after a harsh morning
of rain, the clouds lifted, the wind
fell; there was a resurrection
of nature, and we there to emerge
with it into the anointed
air. I wanted to say to you: 'We
will remember this.' But tenses
were out of place on that green
island, ringed with the rain's
bow, that we had found and would spend
the rest of our lives looking for.

RELAY

I switch on, tune in –
the marvellous languages
of the peoples of the planet,
discussing the weather! Thousands of years
speech was evolving – that line of trees
on the hill slope has the illusion
of movement. I think of man
on his mountain; he has paused
now for lack of the oxygen
of the spirit; the easier options
surround him, the complacencies of being
half-way up. He needs some breath
from the summit, a stench rising
to him from the valley from
which he has toiled to release
his potential; a memory rather
of those bright flags, that other
climbers of other mountains
have planted and gone
their way, not down but on
up the incline of their choosing.

THE PRAYER

He kneeled down
    dismissing his orisons
as inappropriate; one by one
    they came to his lips and were swallowed
but without bile.
    He fell back
on an old prayer: Teach me to know
    what to pray for. He
listened; after the weather of
    his asking, no still, small
voice, only the parade
    of ghosts, casualties
of his past intercessions. He
    held out his hands, cupped
as though to receive blood, leaking
    from life's side. They
remained dry, as his mouth
    did. But the prayer formed:
Deliver me from the long drought
    of the mind. Let leaves
from the deciduous Cross
    fall on us, washing
us clean, turning our autumn
    to gold by the affluence of their fountain.

THE TOOL

So there was nothing?
Nothing. An echo?
Who spoke? There was emptiness
and a face staring, seeking
a likeness. There was thought
probing an absence. God
knew he was naked and
withdrew himself. And the germs
swarmed, their alphabet
lengthened; where was the tongue
to pronounce it? Pain, said
the voice, and the creature
stood up, its mind folded
on darkness. It put out a hand,
as though to implore
wisdom, and a tool
gleamed there. The alternatives
of the tree sharpened. God
spoke to him out of the tree's
wholeness, but the sound
of the tool drowned him. He came forth
in his nakedness. 'Forgive me,'
he said, suffering the tool's
insolence in his own body.

GOOD FRIDAY

It was quiet. What had the sentry
to cry, but that it was the ninth hour
and all was not well? The darkness
began to lift, but it was not the mind

was illumined. The carpenter
had done his work well to sustain
the carpenter's burden; the Cross an example
of the power of art to transcend timber.

POSTE RESTANTE

I want you to know how it was,
whether the Cross grinds into dust
under men's wheels or shines brightly
as a monument to a new era.

There was a church and one man
served it, and few worshipped
there in the raw light on the hill
in winter, moving among the stones
fallen about them like the ruins
of a culture they were too weak
to replace, too poor themselves
to do anything but wait
for the ending of a life
they had not asked for.
                    The priest would come
and pull on the hoarse bell nobody
heard, and enter that place
of darkness, sour with the mould
of the years. And the spider would run
from the chalice, and the wine lie
there for a time, cold and unwanted
by all but he, while the candles
guttered as the wind picked
at the roof. And he would see
over that bare meal his face
staring at him from the cracked glass
of the window, with the lips moving
like those of an inhabitant of
a world beyond this.

And so back
to the damp vestry to the book
where he would scratch his name and the date
he could hardly remember, Sunday
by Sunday, while the place sank
to its knees and the earth turned
from season to season like the wheel
of a great foundry to produce
you, friend, who will know what happened.

WOMAN COMBING
DEGAS

So the hair, too,
        can be played?

She lets it down
        and combs a sonata

from it: brown cello
        of hair, with the arm

bowing. Painter,
        who with your quick

brush, gave us this silent
        music, there is nothing

that you left out.
        The blues and greens,

the abandoned snowfall
        of her shift, the light

on her soft flesh tell us
        from what score she performs.

THE SON

It was your mother wanted you;
you were already half-formed
when I entered. But can I deny
the hunger, the loneliness bringing me in
from myself? And when you appeared
before me, there was no repentance
for what I had done, as there was shame
in the doing it; compassion only
for that which was too small to be called
human. The unfolding of your hands
was plant-like, your ear was the shell
I thundered in; your cries, when they came,
were those of a blind creature
trodden upon; pain not yet become grief.

MEDIATIONS

And to one God says: Come
to me by numbers and
figures; see my beauty
in the angles between
stars, in the equations
of my kingdom. Bring
your lenses to the worship
of my dimensions: far
out and far in, there
is always more of me
in proportion. And to another:
I am the bush burning
at the centre of
your existence; you must put
your knowledge off and come
to me with your mind
bare. And to this one
he says: Because of
your high stomach, the bleakness
of your emotions, I
will come to you in the simplest
things, in the body
of a man hung on a tall
tree you have converted to
timber and you shall not know me.

'I had to do it that way.'
'A god, then, is under constraint?'
'Put it like that, but the material—'
'Whose material?'
                    'You don't understand.
It was always here, a matter
of refinement.'
                    'The dinosaurs,
I suppose!'
            'They were my plough
in the preparation of the earth
for your sowing.'
                    'First seed,
then man! When does a little
become a lot? There was a moment
you recognized me; was I window
or mirror?'
            'You were my waste
of breath, the casualty
of my imagination. But often,
when I would wipe the earth
clean, I remember the patience
of my ploughing, the stubbornness
of the thick soil. It is not bone
that I need now, but the chemistry
of the spirit. The heart has become
hard; I must experiment
with it a little longer in
the crucible of the adult mind.'

THE CHAPEL

A little aside from the main road,
becalmed in a last-century greyness,
there is the chapel, ugly, without the appeal
to the tourist to stop his car
and visit it. The traffic goes by,
and the river goes by, and quick shadows
of clouds, too, and the chapel settles
a little deeper into the grass.

But here once on an evening like this,
in the darkness that was about
his hearers, a preacher caught fire
and burned steadily before them
with a strange light, so that they saw
the splendour of the barren mountains
about them and sang their amens
fiercely, narrow but saved
in a way that men are not now.

THE RECEPTION

The clouds were brown
like the landscape. Sullen men
worked there, fingering their
scars. The brown
got into their minds
so that they could not see
God. It concerned him
at times. He arrayed himself
in bright green, but the winds of that place
burned him; he was a ghost
unnoticed, a body nailed
to a dead tree. When he came down
no one rejoiced; he was as dry leaves
blowing, flimsy integument
of the hard soil.
                  He withdrew to
consider, rejuvenating
himself at the mind's
sources. White, he thought;
I will visit this people
as a white bird, my feathers
their winter. They perceived
him then; fell upon him
in silence, seeking for the brown soil
he deprived them of,
trampling him into it.

THE CASUALTY

I had forgotten
    the old quest for truth
        I was here for. Other cares

held me: urgencies
    of the body; a girl
        beckoned; money

had never appeared
    so ethereal; it was God's blood
        circulating in the veins

of creation; I partook
    of it like Communion, lost
        myself on my way

home, with the varying voices
    on call. Moving backward
        into a receding

future, I lost the use
    of perspective, borrowing poetry
        to buy my children

their prose. The past was a poor
    king, rendering his crown down
        for the historian. Every day

I went on with that
    metallic warfare in which
        the one casualty is love.

THE PROBLEM

There was this problem.
The mind contemplated it;
the body amused itself
in the sun. Put it by, put it by,
the wind whispered. The mind
dozed. Seven empires went under
the blown sand. A people stood up
in Athens; the problem recognized
them, but was not to be outstared
by their blind sculpture. Son of God
or Son of Man? At Jerusalem
the problem was given a new shape.
The Cross offered its gaunt solution
to the Gentiles; under its shadow
their bones whitened. The philosophers christened
their premise. The problem reposed
over the cellars of the alchemists.

PROBING

No one would know you had lived,
but for my discovery
of the anonymous undulation
of your grave, like the early swelling
of the belly of a woman
who is with child. And if I entered
it now, I would find your bones
huddled together, but without
flesh, their ruined architecture
a reproach, the skull luminous
but not with thought.
                  Would it help us to learn
what you were called in your forgotten
language? Are not our jaws
frail for the sustaining of the consonants'
weight? Yet they were balanced
on tongues like ours, echoed
in the ears' passages, in intervals when
the volcano was silent. How
tenderly did the woman handle
them, as she leaned her haired body
to yours? Where are the instruments
of your music, the pipe of hazel, the
bull's horn, the interpreters
of your loneliness on this
ferocious planet?
               We are domesticating
it slowly; but at times it rises
against us, so that we see again
the primeval shadows you built

your fire amongst. We are cleverer
than you; our nightmares
are intellectual. But we never awaken
from the compulsiveness of the mind's
stare into the lenses' furious interiors.

THE FLOWER

I asked for riches.
You gave me the earth, the sea,
                    the immensity
of the broad sky. I looked at them
and learned I must withdraw
            to possess them. I gave my eyes
            and my ears, and dwelt
in a soundless darkness
                    in the shadow
            of your regard.
                        The soul
            grew in me, filling me
with its fragrance.
                    Men came
to me from the four
            winds to hear me speak
            of the unseen flower by which
I sat, whose roots were not
in the soil, nor its petals the colour
of the wide sea; that was
            its own species with its own
            sky over it, shot
with the rainbow of your coming and going.

TOM

In the moment of realizing
it was God looking at him
he became insane. The one man
who could have told us exactly
what he was like was reduced, not
to silence, but to a beast's
idiom. We went up to him
close: 'What was he like?' The brute eyes
swivelled. The arms stretched out; he
became a cross on which memory
suffered. 'What did he say?' 'Yuh,
yuh, yuh.' The saliva babbled
from his slewed mouth. He would hug young
children to death for the love of that God.

SELF-PORTRAIT

That resigned look! Here I am,
it says; fifty-nine,
balding, shirking the challenge
of the young girls. Time running out
now, and the soul
unfinished. And the heart knows
this is not the portrait
it posed for. Keep the lips
firm; too many disappointments
have turned the mouth down
at the corners. There is no surgery
can mend those lines; cruelly
the light fingers them and the mind
winces. All that skill,
life, on the carving
of the curved nostril and to no end
but disgust. The hurrying eyes
pause, waiting for an outdistanced
gladness to overtake them.

FARMING PETER

and there the scarecrow walked
over the surface of the brown
breakers tattered like Christ
himself and the man went
at his call with the fathoms
under him and because
of his faith in the creation
of his own hands he was
buoyed up floundering
but never sinking scalded
by the urine of the skies deaf
to the voices calling from
the high road telling him
his Saviour's face was of straw.

ANN GRIFFITH

So God spoke to her,
she the poor girl from the village
without learning. 'Play me,'
he said, 'on the white keys
of your body. I have seen you dance
for the bridegrooms that were not
to be, while I waited for you
under the ripening boughs of
the myrtle. These people know me
only in the thin hymns of
the mind, in the arid sermons
and prayers. I am the live God,
nailed fast to the old tree
of a nation by its unreal
tears. I thirst, I thirst
for the spring water. Draw it up
for me from your heart's well and I will change
it to wine upon your unkissed lips.

THE MOON IN LLEYN

The last quarter of the moon
of Jesus gives way
to the dark; the serpent
digests the egg. Here
on my knees in this stone
church, that is full only
of the silent congregation
of shadows and the sea's
sound, it is easy to believe
Yeats was right. Just as though
choirs had not sung, shells
have swallowed them; the tide laps
at the Bible; the bell fetches
no people to the brittle miracle
of the bread. The sand is waiting
for the running back of the grains
in the wall into its blond
glass. Religion is over, and
what will emerge from the body
of the new moon, no one
can say.

      But a voice sounds
in my ear: Why so fast,
mortal? These very seas
are baptized. The parish
has a saint's name time cannot
unfrock. In cities that
have outgrown their promise people
are becoming pilgrims
again, if not to this place,

then to the recreation of it
in their own spirits. You must remain
kneeling. Even as this moon
making its way through the earth's
cumbersome shadow, prayer, too,
has its phases.

SUDDENLY

As I had always known
he would come, unannounced,
remarkable merely for the absence
of clamour. So truth must appear
to the thinker; so, at a stage
of the experiment, the answer
must quietly emerge. I looked
at him, not with the eye
only, but with the whole
of my being, overflowing with
him as a chalice would
with the sea. Yet was he
no more there than before,
his area occupied
by the unhaloed presences.
You could put your hand
in him without consciousness
of his wounds. The gamblers
at the foot of the unnoticed
cross went on with
their dicing; yet the invisible
garment for which they played
was no longer at stake, but worn
by him in this risen existence.

THE IN-LAW

Life, too, fights against itself.
The mother-in-law has her revenge
on the son's wife, dragging her
down with her as she goes
into that dark country without love
that marches with the territory
of her frustration. 'She took
him from me. I take her from him
now.' She leans on her, whispering
how good she is, measuring her
for the shroud she is at work upon
with her mind's needle. The girl shines,
carrying herself like that clear
mirror life looks in to see itself torn.

TASTE

I had preferred Chaucer
but for the slop in his saucer;

or grave Edmund Spenser
moving formally as a dancer.

But Shakespeare's cut and thrust,
I allow you, was a must

on my bookshelves; and after,
Donne's thin, cerebral laughter.

Dryden I could not abide,
nor the mincing fratricide

of Pope. Jonathan Swift,
though courageous, had no uplift.

But Wordsworth, looking in the lake
of his mind, him I could take;

and Percy Shelley at times;
Byron, too, but only for his rhymes.

Tennyson? Browning? If I mention
them, it is but from convention,

despite the vowel technique
of the one, the other's moral cheek.

Then Hardy, for many a major
poet, is for me just an old-stager,

shuffling about a bogus heath
cobwebbed with his Victorian breath.

And coming to my own century
with its critics' compulsive hurry

to place a poet, I must smile
at the congestion at the turnstile

of fame, the faceless, formless amoeba
with the secretion of its *vers libre*.

ROUGH

God looked at the eagle that looked at
the wolf that watched the jack-rabbit
cropping the grass, green and curling
as God's beard. He stepped back;
it was perfect, a self-regulating machine
of blood and faeces. One thing was missing:
he skimmed off a faint reflection of himself
in sea-water; breathed air into it,
and set the red corpuscles whirling. It was not long
before the creature had the eagle, the wolf and
the jack-rabbit squealing for mercy. Only the grass
resisted. It used it to warm its imagination
by. God took a handful of small germs,
sowing them in the smooth flesh. It was curious,
the harvest: the limbs modelled an obscene
question, the head swelled, out of the eyes came
tears of pus. There was the sound
of thunder, the loud, uncontrollable laughter of
God, and in his side like an incurred stitch, Jesus.

THE GAP

The one thing they were not troubled
by was perfection; it was theirs
already. Their hand moved in the dark
like a priest's, giving its blessing
to the bare wall. Drawings appeared
there like a violation of the privacy
of the creatures. They withdrew with their work
finished, leaving the interrogation of it
to ourselves, who inherit everything
but their genius.
                This was before
the fall. Somewhere between them and us
the mind climbed up into the tree
of knowledge, and saw the forbidden subjects
of art, the emptiness of the interiors
of the mirror that life holds up
to itself, and began venting its frustration
in spurious metals, in the cold acts of the machine.

THE ANNUNCIATION
BY VENEZIANO

The messenger is winged
                         and the girl
haloed a distance
                  between them
and between them and us
down the long path the door
through which he has not
                           come
on his lips what all women
                   desire to hear
in his hand the flowers that
                  he has taken from her.

IVAN KARAMAZOV

Yes, I know what he is like:
a kind of impossible robot
you insert your prayers into
like tickets, that after a while
are returned to you with the words
'Not granted' written upon them.
I repudiate such a god.
But if, as you say, he exists,
and what I do is an offence
to him, let him punish me;
I shall not squeal; to be proved
right is worth a lifetime's
chastisement. And to have God
avenging himself is to have
the advantage, till the earth opens
to receive one into a dark
cleft, where, safer than Elijah,
one will know him trumpeting
in the wind and the fire
and the roar of the earthquake, but not
in the still, small voice of the
worms that deliver one for ever
out of the tyranny of his self-love.

LIKE THAT

He remembers how younger,
when he was reading about love,
his love would come quietly
to his room to challenge
description, and how he would put
the book down and listen to her
version of it, with rain
falling, perhaps, and the wind loud.

Selah! It is now he who must
go, and from the familiar prose
of her body make his way back
to his book, to the memory
rather of those earlier evenings, when
too willingly he laid it aside.

THE ROUND

In the beginning was the word.
Was the word spoken? There was an echo
surely; and clinging to it the mind
with its reasons. But the sky's face
was unchanged. It was the lesser expressions,
the moon, the domesticity
of the zodiac, it was these accommodated
the man. He fell into the deep sleep
of remembrance, fingering the chord
of his rib, till the music
awoke him: and there at his torn side –
He put out his blunt hand and the fire
kindled, and the many voices of children
called.
      He returned again and again
to be burned, while over him the night drove
with its plough, and the showers of the stars
fell, and the darkness was the face of the god
looking at him without approbation.

HILL CHRISTMAS

They came over the snow to the bread's
purer snow, fumbled it in their huge
hands, put their lips to it
like beasts, stared into the dark chalice
where the wine shone, felt it sharp
on their tongue, shivered as at a sin
remembered, and heard love cry
momentarily in their hearts' manger.

They rose and went back to their poor
holdings, naked in the bleak light
of December. Their horizon contracted
to the one small, stone-riddled field
with its tree, where the weather was nailing
the appalled body that had asked to be born.

THE COMBAT

You have no name.
We have wrestled with you all
day, and now night approaches,
the darkness from which we emerged
seeking; and anonymous
you withdraw, leaving us nursing
our bruises, our dislocations.

For the failure of language
there is no redress. The physicists
tell us your size, the chemists
the ingredients of your
thinking. But who you are
does not appear, nor why
on the innocent marches
of vocabulary you should choose
to engage us, belabouring us
with your silence. We die, we die
with the knowledge that your resistance
is endless at the frontier of the great poem.

SCENES

A relation of mine was in China
at the time. There is a stillness
about certain Ming vases which in itself
is a form of prayer, though to what god
is not known. Sitting in my room
in the sunlight, watching my pulse,
I see that it has the rhythm
of the machine, as there are moments
in a Bach fugue when we are at the centre
of the universe and hear the throb
of the great dynamo that converts
music to power. There is a language
beyond speech we are given to learn
by a suspension of the categories
of the present. Hurrying to and fro
in the imagination, we find its furniture
is of no period, yet all its rooms
blend to accommodate the restlessness
of the spirit. So in the huge night,
awakening, I have re-interpreted
the stars' signals and seen the reflection
in an eternal mirror of the mystery
terrifying enough to be named Love.

FFYNON FAIR
(ST MARY'S WELL)

They did not divine it, but
they bequeathed it to us:
clear water, brackish at times,
complicated by the white frosts
of the sea, but thawing quickly.

Ignoring my image, I peer down
to the quiet roots of it, where
the coins lie, the tarnished offerings
of the people to the pure spirit
that lives there, that has lived there
always, giving itself up
to the thirsty, withholding
itself from the superstition
of others, who ask for more.

SOMEWHERE

Something to bring back to show
you have been there: a lock of God's
hair, stolen from him while he was
asleep; a photograph of the garden
of the spirit. As has been said,
the point of travelling is not
to arrive, but to return home
laden with pollen you shall work up
into the honey the mind feeds on.

What are our lives but harbours
we are continually setting out
from, airports at which we touch
down and remain in too briefly
to recognize what it is they remind
us of? And always in one
another we seek the proof
of experiences it would be worth dying for.

Surely there is a shirt of fire
this one wore, that is hung up now
like some rare fleece in the hall of heroes?
Surely these husbands and wives
have dipped their marriages in a fast
spring? Surely there exists somewhere,
as the justification for our looking for it,
the one light that can cast such shadows?

MARGED

Was she planned?
Or is this one of life's
throw-offs? Small, taken from school
young; put to minister
to a widowed mother, who keeps
her simple, she feeds the hens,
speaks their language, is one
of them, quick, easily
frightened, with sharp
eyes, ears. When I have
been there, she keeps her perch
on my mind. I would
stroke her feathers, quieten
her, say: 'Life is
like this.' But have I
the right, who have seen plainer
women with love
in abundance, with
freedom, with money to
hand? If there is one thing
she has, it is a bird's
nature, volatile
as a bird. But even
as those among whom she
lives and moves, who look at her
with their expectant
glances, song is denied her.

THUS

Whatever you imagine
has happened. No words
are unspoken, no actions
undone: wine poisoned

in the chalice, the corpses
raped. While Isaiah's
angel hither and thither
flies with his hot coal.

SELAH

A procession of honest men
going to their doom, wind-broken
their hands, their dreams withering
behind them like the afterbirth
of a machine. To a hero a
harbour is that which he sets out
from. Is it history that is the salt
in his spittle? We demand our reason
from skies that have the emptiness
of our affirmations. In Israel once
the chastity of the unthinking
body was violated by
the spirit, but the earth had
its revenge; kings opened
their veins over the aridity
of the treaties. The nations proceeded
to the manufacture of the angels
with steel wings, hurrying
to and fro with their unnecessary
message. Beyond the horizons
of our knowledge, in deserts
not of its own making, the self
sought for the purpose that had brought it there.

THE CALLING

And the word came – was it a god
spoke or a devil? – Go
to that lean parish; let them tread
on your dreams; and learn silence

is wisdom. Be alone with yourself
as they are alone in the cold room
of the wind. Listen to the earth
mumbling the monotonous song

of the soil: I am hungry, I
am hungry, in spite of the red dung
of this people. See them go
one by one through that dark door

with the crumpled ticket of your prayers
in their hands. Share their distraught
joy at the dropping of their inane
children. Test your belief

in spirit on their faces staring
at you, on beauty's surrender
to truth, on the soul's selling
of itself for a corner

by the body's fire. Learn the thinness
of the window that is
between you and life, and how
the mind cuts itself if it goes through.

ALIVE

It is alive. It is you,
God. Looking out I can see
no death. The earth moves, the
sea moves, the wind goes
on its exuberant
journeys. Many creatures
reflect you, the flowers
your colour, the tides the precision
of your calculations. There
is nothing too ample
for you to overflow, nothing
so small that your workmanship
is not revealed. I listen
and it is you speaking.
I find the place where you lay
warm. At night, if I waken,
there are the sleepless conurbations
of the stars. The darkness
is the deepening shadow
of your presence; the silence a
process in the metabolism
of the being of love.

THE PRISONER

'Poems from prison! About
what?'

        'Life and God.' 'God
in prison? Friend, you trifle
with me. His face, perhaps,
at the bars, fading
like life.'

        'He came in
with the warder, striving
with him. Where else
did the severity of the man
spring from, but awareness
of a charity he must
overcome?'

        'The blows, then,
were God chastening
the beloved! Who
was the more blessed, the
dispenser or receiver
of them?'

        'It is the same
outside. Bars, walls
but make the perspective
clear. *Deus absconditus!*
We ransack the heavens,
the distance between
stars; the last place we look
is in prison, his hideout
in flesh and bone.'

        'You believe,
then?'

'The poems
are witness. If his world
contracted, it was to give birth
to the larger vision. Not meadows
empty of him, animal
eyes, impersonal
as glass, communicate
God. On the bare walls
of a cell the oppressor watches
the diminishing of his
human shadow, as
he withdraws from the light.'

WHICH

And in the book I read:
God is love. But lifting
my head, I do not find it
so. Shall I return

to my book and, between
print, wander an air
heavy with the scent
of this one word? Or not trust

language, only the blows that
life gives me, wearing them
like those red tokens with which
an agreement is sealed?

GONE

There was a flower blowing
and a hand plucked it.

There was a stream flowing
and a body smirched it.

There was a pure mirror
of water and a face came

and looked in it. There were words
and wars and treaties, and feet trampled

the earth and the wheels
seared it; and an explosion

followed. There was dust
and silence; and out of the dust

a plant grew, and the dew formed
upon it; and a stream seeped

from the dew to construct
a mirror, and the mirror was empty.

PARDON

What pardon for this, Lord?

There was a man ate bread
from your hand and did not snap
at it; but when on his knees
listened to the snivelling sound
of laughter from somewhere inside
himself. He had been taught
that to laugh was an echo
of the divine joy; but this
was the lifting of a dog's leg
in a temple. There is no defence
against laughter issuing
at the wrong time, but is there ever
forgiveness?
        He went from his prayers
into a world holding
its sides, but the return
to them was the return
to vomit, thanking where
he did not believe for something
he did not want but could not
refuse.
     There is no pardon
for this, only the expedient
of blaming the laughter on someone else.

MARRIAGE

I look up; you pass.
I have to reconcile your
existence and the meaning of it
with what I read: kings and queens
and their battles
for power. You have your battle,
too. I ask myself: Have
I been on your side? Lovelier
a dead queen than a live
wife? History worships
the fact but cannot remain
neutral. Because there are no kings
worthy of you; because poets
better than I are not here
to describe you; because time
is always too short, you must go by
now without mention, as unknown
to the future as to
the past, with one man's
eyes resting on you
in the interval of his concern.

MONTROSE

It is said that he went gaily to that scaffold,
dressed magnificently as a bridegroom,
his lace lying on him like white frost
in the windless morning of his courage.

His red blood was the water of life,
changed to wine at the wedding banquet;
the bride Scotland, the spirit dependent on
such for the consummation of her marriage.

CODA

And not refusing
it, indulging in it
rather. All those days
of refreshment; the nights, too,
enormous incinerators
of time. 'Tell me,' the voice
said, and was silent
before the absurdity
of the question.
                There was that
girl in Hawaii, was it,
or Bombay? and only the ocean
between us, that is the gallery
of the drowned, the staircase
we may not climb. The game
is its own rules, the drama
is what the audience is
for. I have come
in my reading of the narrative
of myself to the page
that is not
there, and have put the book down.

THE BRIGHT FIELD

I have seen the sun break through
to illuminate a small field
for a while, and gone my way
and forgotten it. But that was the pearl
of great price, the one field that had
the treasure in it. I realize now
that I must give all that I have
to possess it. Life is not hurrying

on to a receding future, nor hankering after
an imagined past. It is the turning
aside like Moses to the miracle
of the lit bush, to a brightness
that seemed as transitory as your youth
once, but is the eternity that awaits you.

NOW

Men, who in their day
went down acknowledging
defeat, what would they say
now, where no superlatives
have meaning? What was failure
to them, our abandonment
of an ideal has turned
into high art. Could
they with foreknowledge have
been happy? Can we,
because there are levels
not yet descended to,
take comfort? Is it
sufficient for us
that we, like that minority
of our fellows in the hurrying
centuries, turning aside
re-enter the garden? What
is the serenity of art
worth without the angels
at the hot gates, whose sword
is time and our uneasy conscience?

LLANANNO

I often call there.
There are no poems in it
for me. But as a gesture
of independence of the speeding
traffic I am a part
of, I stop the car,
turn down the narrow path
to the river, and enter
the church with its clear reflection
beside it.
        There are few services
now; the screen has nothing
to hide. Face to face
with no intermediary
between me and God, and only the water's
quiet insistence on a time
older than man, I keep my eyes
open and am not dazzled,
so delicately does the light enter
my soul from the serene presence
that waits for me till I come next.

THE INTERROGATION

But the financiers will ask
in that day: Is it not better
to leave broken bank balances
behind us than broken heads?

And Christ recognizing the
new warriors will feel breaching
his healed side their terrible
pencil and the haemorrhage of its figures.

SEA-WATCHING

Grey waters, vast
        as an area of prayer
that one enters. Daily
        over a period of years
I have let the eye rest on them.
Was I waiting for something?
                        Nothing
but that continuous waving
        that is without meaning
occurred.
        Ah, but a rare bird is
rare. It is when one is not looking,
at times one is not there
                    that it comes.
You must wear your eyes out,
as others their knees.
        I became the hermit
of the rocks, habited with the wind
and the mist. There were days,
so beautiful the emptiness
it might have filled,
                its absence
was as its presence; not to be told
any more, so single my mind
after its long fast,
            my watching from praying.

GOOD

The old man comes out on the hill
and looks down to recall earlier days
in the valley. He sees the stream shine,
the church stand, hears the litter of
children's voices. A chill in the flesh
tells him that death is not far off
now: it is the shadow under the great boughs
of life. His garden has herbs growing.
The kestrel goes by with fresh prey
in its claws. The wind scatters the scent
of wild beans. The tractor operates
on the earth's body. His grandson is there
ploughing; his young wife fetches him
cakes and tea and a dark smile. It is well.